# LOOKING ON THE WEBSITE FOR LOVE

Poems

AUTHOR

Hanna Belska

# Looking on the website for love

Copyright © 2014 Hanna Belska

All rights reserved.

No part of this book may be used or reproduced by any means.

Library of Congress Literary Work

U.S. Copy right Office

Case / SR#: 1-1819655053

Case Date: 10/20/2014

Submitted by AASD on 10/21/2014

Title: Looking on the website for love

Library of Congress

Copyright Office - TX

Title ID: 5173432

ISBN-13: 978-0692352915

# Looking on the website for love

Looking on the website for love ............................................................. 6
Adventure with poems ............................................................................. 10
My beginnings of writing poetry ............................................................ 12
Recovered feelings ..................................................................................... 14
I am ................................................................................................................. 16
What matters to me ................................................................................... 18
I asked my angels ........................................................................................ 20
If you knew ................................................................................................... 21
You need to know ....................................................................................... 22
Sing to me ..................................................................................................... 23
He needs to know ....................................................................................... 24
As long as we'll be together ..................................................................... 26
Game called - Questions and Answers ................................................. 28
Let me hear your voice ............................................................................. 30
Reflection of a gloomy mood ................................................................. 36
If you want to be my friend ..................................................................... 37
The invitation to play in words ............................................................... 39
If you want to be mine .............................................................................. 40
Someone like you ....................................................................................... 42
I'm looking for someone .......................................................................... 43
Just for you ................................................................................................... 44
Your sorrows ................................................................................................ 47
From now on ............................................................................................... 49
I Hope ............................................................................................................ 51
What do you want? .................................................................................... 52
Will I ever be able to inspire you ........................................................... 54

# Looking on the website for love

Tell me about yourself
Missing
Tips from Heaven
Surprise for me
About your nights
Prayer to a soldier
Timbre
Scam and Gain
Desperation
You can try
It is not so easy
I will take care
Your intent
What did you gain?
Questionable satisfaction
How much do you need?
He hasn't yet had a chance
My thank you note
Chances of primitive pride
If you think
Your cynicism
Think you were not able
Why are ladies getting a divorce?
When something is lost
Your explanation?
Your opinion

# Looking on the website for love

Your feelings..................................................................................101
Despite the fact that I wish ...........................................102
It is not true ......................................................................103
Questionable reasons for behavior ...........................105

# Looking on the website for love

**Looking on the website for love**

When circumstances make us acknowledge our loneliness making itself
comfortable
at the doors of our everyday life
frightening with emptiness
taking away the desire and impetus for motivation
we begin to look for hope and for a better future
believing somewhere we can find someone to love.

The Internet offers many possibilities
making it easier to look for
and be able to present
to those whose shyness doesn't prevent
taking steps to follow the footsteps of desires.

The Internet provides a field of performances for fraudsters who only
have in mind
not working too hard
to earn as much as possible
as soon as possible
so they try to prey
on the gullibility of those who have no idea
they may fall into the trap of the cheater.

# Looking on the website for love

Scammers can create affection

by promising devotion

to those who are weak, lonely and searching

for love.

Scammers develop affection

in those who feel the need

to have someone close

and in those who believe in good intentions.

Scammers like to promise to the seekers of love

Something that they want

something that is difficult to achieve for themselves.

Those whose loneliness leads to desperate desires

losing caution along the way

allowing them to be drawn into a naive faith

in imaginary love

offered by scammers

who invent stories

only to take advantage of someone's naivety

for their own needs

out of pure greed.

## Looking on the website for love

But there are some

who find their happiness

and are very pleased

that they chose such a path

to find someone close.


Everyone has a chance to look,

it's true

but

there are also those

who seek but don't always want to find -

they are too picky

not wanting to accept what is offered to them

expecting to meet unrealistic dreams.


There are those who place the bar too high

not giving anyone a chance

because they don't want to waste time

on those to whom they don't want to devote more attention

They are in the eternal search of the shadow of their own imagination

which has drifted away from reality.


I also tried to get to know someone in this way

## Looking on the website for love

and my experiences have resulted in the

poems that I present in this book.

# Looking on the website for love

**Adventure with poems**

My adventure with poems

began not so long ago

and arrived

in a strange way

when my daughter received a letter -

I learned

she had sent a poem for a contest

at the age of 13.

When I asked her to read it to me

I couldn't believe

at her age she created completely and casually -

as if most ordinary homework,

a very mature piece.

Her writing impressed me

and at the same time it was able

to sow in me a grain of desire

encouraging me to write.

# Looking on the website for love

If she could at that age

awaken the talent in herself

why couldn't I?

This gave me the idea

that

at least I should try.

# Looking on the website for love

**My beginnings of writing poetry**

After my daughter

fueled in me a desire to write poems

literally a few days after

when I tried to find a boyfriend on a website,

I came across a scammer.

In the first letter

he covered me with words of praise

It sounded strange and suspicious

he didn't know me

and yet he was able to pour deep confessions on the page.

Instead of getting scared and running away

I was in a very strange way inspired with a desire to write.

Although I came across a cheater,

rather than getting angry

I was intrigued and chose to write.

Startled by my own behavior

# Looking on the website for love

I didn't know from where and why

suddenly I was able to

write without major problems and besides

I could put on paper thoughts that flooded me

with a stream of it.

# Looking on the website for love

**Recovered feelings**

For a long time I was convinced -
my feelings departed long ago
when someone didn't care
and stamped upon them carelessly.

I forgot I used to be able to
bestow someone with feelings
despite all
my feelings were still there
only they hid
and I was afraid to reveal them
to allow again
a lack of respect from someone's side
to take away my glow.

I thought and I was convinced -
my feelings passed
and would never return.
Oddly in me a light caught fire

# Looking on the website for love

and showed me the way

to my heart

which was broken and wounded.

The light gave me the strength

so I could warm up

fix and revive my heart

so it could once again send signals,

warming me with a feeling of joy

so I would be

able to open my heart

ready to send signs of happiness

and all because

I have found joy in the transmission of thoughts

and in writing them from my memory.

# Looking on the website for love

I am

I have dark hair and blue eyes

I'm not too tall

I'm not too short

My beauty depends on how

Someone approaches it

To someone I can look like a real beauty,

to others maybe not.

Beauty is only a matter of taste

to someone who pays a lot of attention

to the appearance

I have to admit

I don't care

although I can't say

I ignore the subject

I just don't think

beauty is the most important thing

and I don't have to appeal to all.

Beauty can deceive

# Looking on the website for love

sending on an imaginary island of dreams

Beauty can quickly pass

leaving a shadow of memories

by creating an imaginative duration

of something which passed along

with fleeing time.

# Looking on the website for love

**What matters to me**

What matters to me

is

what someone has to say.

I like

to listen as well as talk

about experiences

and the thoughts that go through the mind.

I have a peaceful soul

which likes to look into the deep alleys

that intrigue me.

In a crowd I don't like to shout

It doesn't bother me

when I go unnoticed.

I gain a glow in the dance

when the music moves my blood in motion

and when the rhythm

# Looking on the website for love

dictates to me

the shape of the music

when I dance it doesn't bother me

if anyone sees me.

I don't display problems on my face

regardless of what the situation

I doused it with a gentle smile

and when the moment will bring a tear to my eye

I don't hide

because even a tear is unable to break me.

I believe in myself

I also know I can count

on myself

because I like to keep the word

not only to myself.

# Looking on the website for love

*I asked my angels*

I asked my angels to bring me a song from heaven

I had to wait a very long time

and in the end

I received permission to sing.

I am glad

I finally I received this gift

which has waited for me to reach it

if only I had known earlier

I could have sung before.

So now I will not wait any longer

I will sing

and hope

there is someone who will understand

and hear

what I want to tell.

# Looking on the website for love

**If you knew**

If you knew you'd understand

what love really is about.

If you knew

you wouldn't care about facade

you would know

love is made in heaven

if you knew

you would not care about the illusion

and appearances created just to show

painted on the outside with the cover of falsehood

to mask the emptiness inside.

If you knew

you would be intoxicated by the splendor

of the shining rainbow

created only for you

in the way intoxicating dreams

paint images

making easier

to look into depths

of the invisible beauty outside.

# Looking on the website for love

**You need to know**

You must know

I asked the angels

to spare me from those

who are shallow and superficial.

I asked the angels

to spare me

from those who need only a glance

to assess anyone.

I don't need anyone

who thinks only of trinkets and glitter

I need someone who

will be able to tune into their own senses

allowing us to

communicate without any problem

by fine-tuning the wave of mutual understanding

in order to stay in relationship of consenting hearts.

This is what I'm looking for.

# Looking on the website for love

### Sing to me

If you are the one who wants the second heart

sing lyrics for me,

lyrics

magnetized with magic

charming the senses

raising them

to the gates of eternal enchantment.

Listen to my songs

and sing

when I hear your voice

I will know

you are just chanting for me

until then I will be singing

and I will be waiting

until you

begin singing for me.

# Looking on the website for love

**He needs to know**

Only one out there is made only for me

but

he needs to know

what

I'm looking for.


My guy must be only for me

he needs to hear my voice

and understand my songs

written only for him


When I will hear his voice

I'll know

he is the one who I have been looking for

and then I will not care about

how he looks

or what goods he has

I will only celebrate his voice

when he will sing

lyrics sent from heaven

only for me.

# Looking on the website for love

When I will hear his voice

I will rise up

grabbing him behind.

# Looking on the website for love

*As long as we'll be together*

I would like to

dance with you

in the same rhythm and at the same rate

even if this would be

on the ice skating rink

I wouldn't care.

I wouldn't care

If It would rain

I wouldn't care

As long as we would walk together

under the same cover.

I wouldn't be afraid

of any storm

as long as you would brighten

the next day for me

with your smile.

# Looking on the website for love

I would go with you everywhere.

far and high

I wouldn't get tired at all

to keep up with you

to follow your step as long as you

wouldn't be afraid to walk by my side

I may climb as high as you want to.

If only with you

I will not be afraid to fall

If you will help me

to get up quickly

We will do everything we want to,

and whatever we will dream of

as long as we are together.

# Looking on the website for love

Game called - Questions and Answers

I wonder if there are many adventurers
who would trouble,
to start the game of words with me
just for fun and to cheer up a little.
I'm looking for someone,
who will answer my questions
who will ask me questions
who will ask me to deal with some tasks
someone who will listen to answers
with joy and interest.

If anyone wants to cheer themselves
and me
challenge me and I will challenge you
with questions and riddles
I'm looking for those
who want to take on the game with me.

I like to deal with tasks
I like to overcome obstacles

# Looking on the website for love

I'm looking for someone

who can answer my questions

Someone who wants to ask me their own

Someone who will give me a task to resolve.

With joy and attention

I want to seek information

for questions which I have not yet heard

To find the wisdom and knowledge

by searching for answers

just for fun and the joy of discovery.

Then challenge me and I will challenge you.

# Looking on the website for love

*Let me hear your voice*

I don't know why
I feel like I know you
but truth be told
I don't know you at all.

If you can
please introduce yourself
Tell me a little about your dreams
plans and hopes
especially on the road where you choose
to find your match
by searching on a dating site.
What are your expectations
What is your perfect woman
How does she look?

Whether she be beautiful and young
without a gram of fat on her sides
and without a single wrinkle on her face

# Looking on the website for love

or maybe you want her to be covered with a mass of powder

to hide deficiencies

only to present herself well,

to mislead from afar.

Or maybe you prefer

someone who doesn't pretend to be someone else

to please others.

Someone not afraid to be oneself

Someone who doesn't need to mislead

and play games

and not afraid of rejection

when someone finds her unappealing

and doesn't like her.

Let me hear your voice

tell me what you really need

what you really look to find

whether someone with a sincere heart

who will care about you

and dispel your concerns and worries

or maybe someone who brings you nothing but trouble

Someone whose greatest concern is

# Looking on the website for love

to look good in front of others.

Someone whose greatest concern is to please others.

Let me hear your voice

what you really need

and what you are really searching.

What counts most for you in life

something that remains

and lasts a long time

or something that passes through and escapes.

Do you need someone you can count on and trust

or do you need someone who

is counting on you and others

or maybe you need someone

who should get something

only because she deserves it

because she is unique and special

without any major reason

just because.

Trying to maintain the illusion

and cherish the memory of youth

# Looking on the website for love

only because it is with you

without feeling the need to give anything in return.

Whether you are looking for a true partner

who will always be there for you no matter what the situation

and will find time for your needs.

or maybe you need a beautiful symbol

you would present with dignity.

So you can shine

and walk proudly at her side

for show

for others to admire you

and be jealous of you.

Let me hear your voice

what do you need

what you are really looking for.

Do you know what you want

Do you need time

can you give someone time

to allow a chance to get to know each other,

whether in a second

## Looking on the website for love

you know everything within someone -

what hides inside

and in seconds

you are able to know someone's soul

in order to accept

or reject without hesitation

because you don't like

how she looks

and without a greater need to hear her voice

or get to know her.

Without hesitation you are blindly able to reject someone

because you don't like how she looks

and you are sure at once

she isn't the one

You are looking for and waiting for.

Blindly you will strike out your chances of knowing someone

because you have your vision

and your pride

and you know yourself best

What and whom you want

what you really need to be happy.


I want to know

# Looking on the website for love

if you're worth any trouble and effort
to give you some time
to make you smile
to fulfill your soul with joy
and bring happiness to your heart.

Let me hear your voice
to see if you are shallow
or if you are the kind of guy
worth fighting for.

Let me hear your voice
let me hear what you really need
what you are looking for
simply to be happy.

# Looking on the website for love

### Reflection of a gloomy mood

I want to apologize for my words
I'm sure I made you mad
I chose the wrong words.
Looks like I was not in the right mood.
I don't know why I sent you the expression of
my gloomy feelings
I shouldn't have passed them on to you
I don't have intentions
of discouraging you
after all I don't know you.

# Looking on the website for love

**If you want to be my friend**

I don't expect much
and don't offer much
I don't know much about you.

If you want to be my friend
it would be nice
if you want to talk
I sincerely invite you.

If you want to talk
I am ready to listen and respond.

I will talk to you with pleasure
so I am inviting you to play with words.

I need a friend to play with words
I am inviting you only if you want to
think you're ready and able

## Looking on the website for love

to have fun playing with words

I am looking for a partner

who can inspire me

who would know how to play with words.

# Looking on the website for love

**The invitation to play in words**

I hope you will find the courage

to write me a few words-

What do you have to lose.

I don't know you

you don't know me

we can say what we want

without fear that someone will laugh.

I invite you

I think you have

and will find

something to inspire yourself.

This is only innocent play

which can only bring satisfaction

You certainly will not get hurt

So write something

about your hopes and dreams.

# Looking on the website for love

*If you want to be mine*


I'm peace walking in the clouds of hope

Waiting for love and happiness

Waiting and believing

love still exists

Somewhere in the sky up high

I have not stopped believing

I will reach the stars of heaven.


If you want to be mine

you have to be smart and bright

you must be honest.

My heart has to smile when you're around

you need to have a soul of a bird happy and free

Ready to be with me.


If you want to be mine

you have to make me believe

your smile is true and honest

your heart is open and healed

ready to grab me and hold me tight.

# Looking on the website for love

If you want to be mine

you have to make me believe

your soul is ready to fly with mine

and your mind is free, clean and clear

to deal with someone like me

someone who is free from other beliefs

someone who is strong

someone who can fly

even when sitting hard as a rock on the ground

if you want to be mine?

# Looking on the website for love

*Someone like you*

I'm the one

I am nothing less nothing more,

true, loyal and peaceful

for many years I was looking for

someone special who could be for me only

someone loving and devoted in affection

someone mature and wise

from whom I could get advice

who I could admire

who will stand for me,

protect and love me

because there is nothing better than the feeling of happiness when we

are loved

and when we can love in return.

I'm looking for someone who can charm me

touch my heart

and release my soul from longing for

Someone like you.

# Looking on the website for love

**I'm looking for someone**

I'm looking for someone

who will enchant

by touching my heart,

free my soul from yearning

someone with a cheerful breeze

who will reach

straight through my senses.

# Looking on the website for love

Just for you

My heart was empty waiting for you
My wings were tired waiting for you
Just for you
When you see my wings
Just wait
When you see my tears,
Just be patient
When you hear my voice
Just sing for me
The song of love and hope
When you are next to my heart
Just tell me what you feel
Just for me.

When you let me believe
you found love just for me
I will be grateful for you
faithful only to you
I will drop my guards
only for you.

I will be for you

# Looking on the website for love

whenever you call

Whenever you want to

I will be for you

My heart was lonely

waiting for you

only for you.

When you will let me open my wings

I will fly with joy around you

I will spread them

Only for you

To love, hug and protect you,

to take care of you.

When you will help me

open my heart

When you find love

only for me

my heart will be for you

only for you.

When I believe you

I will guide you through the light

# Looking on the website for love

I will guide you through the dark

On the clouds of happiness

I will hold you safe on the chain woven from love

I will bring you harmony

And I will bring you peace

Just let me believe

And let me be

I will fight for you

And I will fly for you

Just for you

Nothing can stop me.

I will be giving and sharing a smile on my face

With my happy eyes

For more than just for you

I will be sharing my love and happiness

for all, only because of you

Just for you.

# Looking on the website for love

### Your sorrows

You went through a lot in your life

it seems it's still not the end

of your sorrows

but

you can be calm and still be strong

as long as it takes to return safely home.

Someone close to you will be with you

to give you strength to go on

to help you survive the grief,

longing and mourning

for those whom you have lost

for those who are gone forever.

Someone close to you will lead you to peace

and

to the end of your despair

will constantly be at your side,

when you need

Someone's heart will weep with you

until this nightmare is over

but don't worry - you will survive

## Looking on the website for love

because you will be strong and resistant

as long as you think

what tomorrow may bring

because God gives strength to those

who are not afraid to move forward.

Someone close to you will encircle you with a magical shield

to protect you from the darkness

from suffering

because you have to come back

happily and safely

therefore you will also gain strength

and faith

and you'll be okay.

# Looking on the website for love

**From now on**

From now on, you don't need to mislead me

and you can't lie to me

you can be honest

and you don't have to hide

the truth from me about your pain

you don't have to be afraid

you will lose me on the way.

You don't have to worry

when you are truthful with me

I will guide you every step of the way

of our journey

You will not be alone

you'll have me

to occupy your mind

to distract you from the tribulations of reality.

Only when you don't fail me

I will be next to you until the end

Only then

# Looking on the website for love

If you will not tell me more lies

then

you can be yourself

because for me it is what I like

and what I admire most.

Even when you are in pain

I can see you and feel your love and your joy of life

you cherish with excitement

and you don't allow it to

be taken away from you

and above all

You don't allow your spirit to be broken

All this is

because

you are blessed in heaven.

# Looking on the website for love

### I Hope

I hope -

you will not let me go,

and not take the easy way out

like lyrics of the song you sent to me

I hope you don't think about the easy way out

leaving me with no other choice.

I waited long for someone

and I don't want you to go

and I don't want you to take

the easy way out

and just go

because we would never know.

For you, the easy way out

is

To stay where you are

but then we would never know?

# Looking on the website for love

What do you want?

If the truth be told
I don't know what to think
whether you can answer me honestly
In your own words.

What are you really looking for?
What do you want?
What are you expecting from a woman?
Can you be as honest and faithful as I am?
As you promised?

I will quietly wait for the answer.
Whether I am the woman
you've been waiting for and dreamed of
If I am the one -
you wanted for a long time
I only want the truth.

Where should I go
do you want me to continue encircled in the clouds
of the sky
or do you want me to go into the blue distance.

# Looking on the website for love

Where should I go

do you want to trim my wings

or maybe

do you want to rise up with me forever

only when you will be true to me?

# Looking on the website for love

Will I ever be able to inspire you

Will I ever be able to inspire you

where you will be able to go on your own

where you will be able to grow

your own feathers on your wings

which will guide you

to your own land of dreams

where you will be wrapped in

the rainbow of floating stars

which you will touch

and you will delight

where every color of the peaceful land will give you a sign

of wisdom and satisfaction.

If ever I'll inspire you

so you will not need to use others

for confidence and for protection,

you must know

you have it in you

# Looking on the website for love

to make your own steps

and to paint in the colors

of your own inspirational palette -

You just have to believe

you have it in you

to give rein to your imagination

to follow your dreams.


If ever I'll inspire you

you will visualize your designs in your sleep

painted with the colors of rainbow stars

and ever

you will not want those

images to leave.


If ever I'll inspire you

we will go together to the future

on the steps of our sweet ballads

upwards through gentle passions

and our beautiful imagination.

# Looking on the website for love

**Tell me about yourself**

Tell me a little about yourself - what do you like?
would you like to be sad a lot?
or would you like to be happy for no reason
what makes you laugh?
I want to know everything about
what you like about yourself
whether or not you hate
everything that makes you tearful
how you stand the pain
and if you can be brave
to face all things unwanted
and not invite trouble
which grows and emerges.


I want to know how smart you are
what do you know and what do you want to know
about life and about yourself
what are your interests
and what brings you pleasure.


I want to know how you think and what you think
about the world which surrounds you

# Looking on the website for love

I also want to know what you believe and if you believe

in the sun bringing you the energy of life

If you have a lot of inexhaustible

and indefatigable power

or if easily you tire and give up fast.

I want to know if you know what brings you joy

if often you are angry without reason

Or if you are calm and quiet

Whether you're a demon of the requirements and demands.

Do you like to be angry and hold onto spite

Do you forgive and forget quickly

Are you able to forget bad memories

or you're the king of mildness and calmness

or the holder of terror

if you like being envious of the goods of others

whether you are sufficiently confident of your own values

or if you like to be unsure of yourself to have a reason to

be uncertain and jealous.

I want to know what you think about

and how you approach money

Does it mean the whole world to you?

## Looking on the website for love

I only want to know what you value the most in your life

and what you care about

What your dreams are

What your plans are

I want to know it all and more

please answer me what you can and what you want

if you want me to know you.

# Looking on the website for love

### Missing

I want to tell you

I miss

I miss the breeze of your messages

When I wake up and when I see

Your selection of words

It makes my day

Fills me with joy,

difficult to identify and define

and most importantly it gives me inspiration

Writing poems

and transmitting my thoughts

because you know how to touch my senses

and how to communicate with me

From a far distance.

# Looking on the website for love

**Tips from Heaven**

Many years ago in my dream
four angels came to me
to give me some tips,
they showed me what to do
and what I have to look for
they showed me
how to close the door behind someone
they told me
to look for someone else.

Much time passed before I understood and realized
what the angels told me.

What they were asking me
took me a long time to do
because even then
I didn't understand
and I did not listen
so my guardian angels flew away
keeping their distance from me
patiently waiting to see what I would do.

# Looking on the website for love

They left only one hint

that

I should look

for another guy

there are many guys

so this hint didn't tell me much

I waited and I hoped

my angels would return

but they will not be rushed and didn't come until

I had received a letter.

They came back with a special touch

and heaven has spoken to me again

They came to me with a unique gift

A gift from the angels.

They dropped a magic feather which turned into a writing pen

which was able to write

and if you ask me why

I got the pen which landed in my hand I wouldn't know the answer.

But I can tell you what I feel

I feel blessed

that my angels came back

# Looking on the website for love

and they are speaking to me again

I am also lucky

they returned with a gift for me

a mouth full of stars

that shine in my presence.


And if you still have doubts

why they touched me right now

you will have to ask my angels

why?

maybe they will tell you

the same they told me

and maybe they will be able to touch you

same as they touched me

You don't have to listen

but if you want to listen to serenade

while they sing for me,

you will hear them and

know why I feel what I feel.


Surprise for me



This morning

# Looking on the website for love

someone rang my bell once

and

when I got to my door

nobody was there

and already

was gone.

At the door I found a note

to pick up a package.

I didn't know who

would send me something

and

I didn't have time

to go and see from whom the parcel could be

when I had time I called the number

I could see on the piece of paper

left for me

by the messenger

to find out

that

if I have time

I can pick it up now

and when I got there

## Looking on the website for love

a surprise was waiting for me,

a surprise which came straight

from you to me

a box of nice flowers

in a vase

It waited for me to open and rejoice.

I want to thank you

and I want to send you back my smiles

which you placed on my face

therefore

thank you once again with a smile

And joy, which you have placed in my heart.

# Looking on the website for love

**About your nights**

Another day without a word from you

Makes me wonder

If you are safe and sound

Where are you?

How do you cope

with your nights?

What do they look like there?

and

how can you still find time for your hopes

and dreams when you are in a sleep?

I'm interested

and if you can, I want to know

if you have a time of peace

When you sleep

without the ringing in your ears from the sound of explosions

surrounding you

I would like to know

if your nightmares come to life

When you sleep

# Looking on the website for love

or

if you can stun them and disable them like a switch.

I would be happy if you

would be able to

say

You don't have to worry,

however it seems that it is impossible

to hear these words

from you

until you return back home

to safety and health.

Until then I will worry and I will pray

for you and your friends

to show that you

are successfully on your way home

and until then

You can count on my prayers.

# Looking on the website for love

**Prayer to a soldier**

I wanted to send you a prayer

charged with love

for you to find peace on the road of life

which you yourself have chosen

long ago as your path to follow.


To stand up for others

to give your own freedom and your everyday life

for those in need

I'm sending you a prayer

loaded with faith

from me to you

to be used as you want

and as you wish.


Faith in love and a better tomorrow

faith that will carry you back home,

to a better future.


I am sending you a prayer steeped

with my warmth

# Looking on the website for love

to give you a special touch

that you are wanted and expected,

to give you a special feeling

that someone is missing you

and can't wait to see you,

someone from a distance,

because you are not alone in this world.

I am sending you a prayer

shining with hope

that everything you do

will bring a better future for others

and your dedication will pay off

and others will not have to suffer anymore

and all this because

you once had a dream to become a soldier.

# Looking on the website for love

**Timbre**

People are speaking and I can't hear
what they want to tell me

In my ears I hear only your voice
What are you saying to me?
and what do you sing to me?

People are trying to repeat to me
what they want me to hear from them
and I still can't hear
what they are saying,
in my ears I hear only your words.

What are you saying to me?
No one's voice is able to muffle
and drown out
this sound
people screaming
to let me know
but I can't hear and still don't understand

## Looking on the website for love

what they want from me.

I only hear the ring of your voice

telling me,

spreading the love

you have for me.

# Looking on the website for love

### Scam and Gain

I don't know why you do what you do
Maybe I got caught on some
kind of scam
and I really don't know
what you want to achieve by this.

But you need to know
The profit is mine
and I gain more.

This type of scam I don't mind
as long as it's only verbal deception
I gain the satisfaction and joy
and I am still gaining
fun in writing and transmitting my thoughts
with happy feelings.
So if you want to fool me again
and more
I will not be complaining
With pleasure I will take

# Looking on the website for love

what you have for me

and you

you can fool me again

but now I must go.

# Looking on the website for love

**Desperation**

You're so desperate to find someone
you just don't know when to stop.

You check many possibilities
and it is hard for you to make up your mind
and figure out which
is the right one for you.

You can lie,
without blinking an eye
you can create stories
which are hard to believe
and still you don't stop
Even when caught in the act.

# Looking on the website for love

*You can try*

You are the one

who helped me discover

how to press

the key to my mind

and my imagination

which allowed me to

become who I always wanted to be

to allow my soul

to break free from blockages

and be able to pass

and express myself

without a shadow of a doubt.

So I could say what I want

to the rest of the world

and feel what I feel

about the rest of the world.

I hope you don't mind hearing

about my benefits

# Looking on the website for love

which I am gladly telling you.

Please don't do the same to someone else

because I may do what someone else

would be unable to do without fear

of getting hurt.

I'm strong enough

and I'm not afraid

so, please

bring me more if you want your imaginary stories

collected and copied from others.

Only I would like to know

what you have to gain

but I am afraid

I can't give you what you're looking for

If I could

I might,

but I'm afraid

I can't give you anything more

than what I have offered to you.

# Looking on the website for love

**It is not so easy**

Do not think

it's so easy to fool me

just because I let

the rein of your imagination go wherever

you wanted to go

to meet your needs

which led you

until I realized

you wanted to deceive me

with more than words alone

As I told you earlier,

when I find out

someone wants to use me,

I will fly away.

So I'm doing it now

and I wish you good luck.

# Looking on the website for love

*I will take care*

If you will be for me

I

will stand forever by your side

If you will never

deceive me

or put me down

I will continue and I will take care of you

regardless of the situation.

I will still be on your side

for better or for worse

but if you lose my faith

then I will get scared and fly away

because I am like an alert animal

trusting and naive

until someone

takes my illusion away from me

and then I'll be a closed like hard stone

resistant to sigh and memory.

# Looking on the website for love

### Your intent

Don't be fooled by my trust and gullibility

I gave you many signs about my doubts

and you chose to be blind and deaf

because you had only one thing

on your mind

to deceive me

and you heard only one voice

your own.

You chose to be deceitful without compunction

for my feelings

because you had only one thing

on your mind.

# Looking on the website for love

What did you gain?

I gave you many signs about my doubts
but you wanted to continue your deception
you didn't have anything
to answer
when I asked.

I asked many questions and you
said nothing or lied to me
thinking that was enough for me
so I can move on and believe you
without any doubts and concerns.

I asked you many questions
and I didn't insist
when you didn't answer me
and you chose silence.

# Looking on the website for love

I asked you many questions

even when I knew the answers

and you still chose to lie to me

and didn't care if I suspected anything.

If I knew your intentions

How hurdy-gurdy

you repeated own words

to make sure

I would hear

what you had for me in the plan.

If you could hear something more than your own voice

then you would have known earlier

you had chosen the wrong way

I only want to know.

What did you gain?

# Looking on the website for love

## Questionable satisfaction

What do you have to gain

when you are looking to deceive,

promising love and devotion,

promising fulfillment to someone with expected

feelings and anticipated dreams?

Do you think this is the way

to wealth and satisfaction?

How long and how far can you carry?

How long and how far will the strategic projections ride

on lies and scams

feeding on someone's love and gullibility?


Do you really think this is the way

to reach the peaks

and climb to the tops of satisfaction?


What kind of joy is created

from someone's weaknesses and someone's tears

when leaving someone

with a broken heart?

## Looking on the website for love

How many hearts have you left behind

disgruntled and distressed

when you stole away

hope of love and joy,

blocking the possibility

for the future and desire to seek,

discouraging further attempts

Leaving behind disgust

taking away the faith in a better future

giving doubts that someone with a good heart

may no longer exist.

# Looking on the website for love

*How much do you need?*

How much money do you need?
How much do you want
my dear?
How much do you think your fraud is worth?

To ask a woman for money
where is your dignity and pride?

Your story from the start made no sense
When you asked for money to bring money
Where is the sense?
Do you really believe
I am so naive?
Do you really think
I bought your fraud?
You should give me more credit
Had you listened to my poems
you would
really know
You have not met a fool
after all I gave you many hints in them

# Looking on the website for love

where my mind is

I must tell you

My mind is made up and straight,

my dear.

There is no money from me to you,

dear

to become my husband I need a little

more than a nonsensical lie

To call me your wife you would have to be honest and true first a man of

honor.

If my husband would be true

Then I would have no problem helping him

and I wouldn't mind

sending him money

if only he would be true

but you are more real than him

therefore I have to go

and you should search for your earnings

in a fair way somewhere else.

# Looking on the website for love

**He hasn't yet had a chance**

I loved

I love and I will love

the man from my imagination.

You know how to create

the someone who was always in my mind

and you know how to help me open my heart

To call for him.

I was sending love letters to you

I created and intended my love

You know that

he exists somewhere for me.

You were smart to create my type of man

perfect for me

if he were only real.

I wouldn't mind sending my letters to you I wrote for him

which he has had no opportunity to receive

Messages from me

# Looking on the website for love

because it seems

I was sending them to the wrong address

and he hadn't had a chance to hear my voice

which I began to chant towards you.

The right man for me is still waiting for me to write -

Everything you wrote sounded

too good to be true

despite the fact that

from the beginning

I saw you had some other intentions towards me.

I didn't know where your plans would go

your world was not known to me

but slowly piece by piece

I was able to gather in the entire image

and you can't fool me anymore.

# Looking on the website for love

**My thank you note**

You unintentionally, despite your other designs,

reverted to enliven something in me

you have turned the switch back on

the switch to create.


I let you fool me because I was afraid

the switch would turn off if I let you go

For a very long time I didn't know what was hiding in me

If not for you I still wouldn't know

when I got the gift

which I didn't know how to use,

and for that I must thank you because I didn't know

that you would appear in my life.

I didn't know if I would pass through my life

not knowing whether I would waste my gift.


So I am sending you a note with my thanks

For the fact

you helped me to find my gift in me

which hid for a long time in front of me.

# Looking on the website for love

### Chances of primitive pride

I don't know what you want to achieve

and who you want to win

thanks to

what you wrote.


You are dreaming of returning to the real matrix

only if you can accurately

pinpoint it

without offending others

without displaying primitive traits of your character.


Memories of pain from the past

shouldn't be a reason to put up barricades

that overwhelm you

and in no way allow you to move forward.


It seems you want to build

your future on the ashes of the past

for which you'll need a lot of luck.

# Looking on the website for love

**If you think**

If you think

You need only look

before you know a situation,

putting someone on a pedestal

or in the basket of your consciousness

you're mistaken

Without reason

some argue that -

in order to get to know a man well

eating a barrel of salt is not enough.


It may be that

your experiences have taught you

to restrict your view

but this will only increase your struggling

which you couldn't see previously

or protect yourself from

allowing your pride to judge others

not giving yourself time to get to know someone better.

## Looking on the website for love

With such a method

you increase your chances

of finding the masked truth

which is much easier

to enchant you with the magnet of duplicity.

# Looking on the website for love

### Your cynicism

I'm not sure about your cynicism -

whether it's only the brilliance of your mind

or whether it's something

that could be called fun

at the expense of others.

What makes you throw needlessly on others

your own frosty dose of cynicism,

molded with snow balls

which I hope

however

quickly dissolve

on the meadows of a peaceful approach

to those who will be able to

with their own wisdom

ignore your irony

by not giving you a reason for satisfaction

to provoke you to continue poking

fun at the expense of someone else

where you like to search for someone's disability

to denude them.

# Looking on the website for love

*Think you were not able*

Thank you for not being

able to introduce yourself

when you sent a few words to me earlier.


It's probably the reason

I don't treat

words from you too seriously

because it looked

as though you had not devoted more attention

when you wrote to me

writing very superficially and perfunctorily

as if you didn't care.


Whether someone

at the very beginning can

or is not able to introduce himself

says little about the man.


It is a pity

that from the beginning

you couldn't take advantage of the opportunity

to modestly introduce yourself to me

# Looking on the website for love

to give me an understanding

that I am dealing with someone

who knows how to respect others.

# Looking on the website for love

## Why are ladies getting a divorce?

In response to the question of a certain gentleman.

Today ladies are getting a divorce
but back in those days they had to give a lot to each other:
work, raise children
and look after the other half
but for themselves there was not enough time.

If they encountered a partner
who could not appreciate
and still complained,
showing eternal dissatisfaction,
nothing else remained
They had to go their own way
where they are able to find peace
and more time for themselves.

Women these days need a partner,
a lover and friend
not a teacher or supervisor

# Looking on the website for love

to which, unfortunately, men are inclined

What probably they inherited from the past

In reality

Who knows - why?

# Looking on the website for love

**When something is lost**

When something is lost
It is easier to appreciate what we had before
and when we go through life alone
it is much easier to understand
why it didn't work when we had the chance
although it seemed like
it was the best
even when the other side had a completely different feeling.

If only one of the parties is able to understand why
and learn
what was a bad experience in the past
it can still be reversed –
everything for a better tomorrow
because everything is in the hands of the future.

Who knows how life will turn out
When we are aware of what
We did in the past what we should not have done.

# Looking on the website for love

Your explanation?

You say

you have explained what you're looking for

and it is true your writing says a lot.

Although

in your writing it's not difficult to see your talent

which I sincerely appreciate

However

speaking about what you're looking for

you enter the reader into an enigmatic world

of entanglement

where even your name is simplified

at the same time

complex and unknown

where it's difficult to follow your thoughts

which pile up in columns

tangled in the lines of otherness

where it's difficult to combine words

to close them together.

You have asked for opinions

so I'll answer

# Looking on the website for love

If you want to be avant-garde

tossing your thoughts on the wall of the prism

I don't have anything against it

I just don't understand

and it's difficult for me to capture the essence

and your reflected

thoughts are not easy for me to catch

because they spray in all directions.

If you are amused and it's your style

this is OK

As long as you're having fun and you create

I appreciate your hard work and effort.

# Looking on the website for love

### Your opinion

Your opinion

is a matter of assessment

to which as anyone you are entitled

I personally don't like in any way an exaggeration

As they say less is more.

I like to draw morals from my stories

regardless of whether they are the ones I write

or the ones I read.

You prefer to pamper your words

by tangling words

What gives a greater stimulus

than simple communication?

I don't call myself an artist

because it is big and small at the same time

only the word

I just have a sensitive soul

I express my opinion

and I respond to a posed question.

## Looking on the website for love

Calling oneself an artist commits

you as an artist,

you want to leave the room for interpretation

to mobilize others to think.

However, I am not able to understand

what you want to convey

although I try the best I can

with tension in my intelligence.

Maybe your art is designed

for someone wiser

Simply I'm not able to understand

such an artist like you

I'm also not sure if you understand yourself

living in limbo

incoming waves of inspiration

provoking their delusions.

This is only my opinion

Maybe you want to share

and lighten my naive look?

# Looking on the website for love

### Your feelings

You write you don't feel
To be able to feel anything
One must put pink sunglasses on
to dim the harsh rays of pride
which like to shine from high
rekindling the fires of disdain
which you don't want to hide from those
who according to you
are not at the same level
of your planetary system.

I am above your standards
and in my world
everything is possible
because I don't close and cut myself off
by putting up barricades
to become isolated from the upcoming trials of life.

Life is too beautiful and too short
to close it in the templates
of our own limitations.

# Looking on the website for love

*Despite the fact that I wish*

Although I would like to share
all that I have to offer
Although I miss having someone close
who would
embrace me with caring wings
however impatient
not rushing me
so I can get just what I expect
I have learned to wait patiently
and it doesn't scare me
if I can't get what I expect.

Although
I miss someone special
the one unique one
doesn't need to be that much for me.

It will be enough for me
when he will be warm enough
so I feel pulses of his faster heartbeat
which could warm my yearning desire.

# Looking on the website for love

**It is not true**

It is not true
I don't know what I want
I know well what I need
what I expect
I know well what I have
what I can and what I want to offer.

I don't like to advertise
or waste time on those
who I could attract and not have time.

I am looking for someone who is not chasing pretenses
to shine in front of others
I need someone who can unleash his own thoughts
from rigid stereotypes
to build a future with me
with youthful enthusiasm.

I am looking for someone who is not tied up
in the race of everyday life
moving on wind-up visions of one's own needs
following the pleasures of sight

# Looking on the website for love

and not allowed to stop.

I need someone who

could with abandon be awakened from pain,

past concerns

and trust me

with naive consciousness

so we could travel to the land

of colorful dreams

so we could bring a smile of joy

and climb

achieving what we want.

Is there someone

who doesn't fear the risks

and is able to abandon the rigidly delineated vision

which supports his own needs?

Is there anyone able to

stand on my doorstep

someone who before he

starts knocking on my door

lays bare of his pride

to free himself from any ballasts.

# Looking on the website for love

Questionable reasons for behavior

If you want to respond with incomprehensible behavior

you have the right to do so

Maybe you think it is ok

to make the appeal that you are oversensitive

because of your previous experience?

I wrote my poem,

because it can be useful for someone

If not for me

it can help you a little

so you will know.

I don't know if you will pick up

all the pieces of your heart

or if it's definitely healed

and whether healed scars

don't hurt you with the changing of the weather?

Is your heart ready

for these solar and cloudy days?

## Looking on the website for love

Do you think it is possible to go past summer

without a storm or rain?

Just as in any relationship

there are changes of moods

if you're not able to put on boots and use an umbrella

in order to bravely be able to face changes

in the weather

I don't know how you can wander anywhere this way

and not let the weather constitute obstacles for you?

The choice is yours

Although,

it looks like you move forward blindly

with your immature behavior.

Do you want to react this way?

Maybe you want to give fate a chance?

Or perhaps you want obstacles to grow in your way

Emotional memories from the past

which always give you a reason to doubt?

Maybe at some point you want to stop

and not let your life pass away

waiting and searching?

# Looking on the website for love

If you want to behave like that

and look for an excuse to feel offended

Unfortunately there's nothing anybody can do

However

you can still change your way

if you are able to understand

what is obvious to others.

www.ingramcontent.com/pod-product-compliance
Lightning Source LLC
Chambersburg PA
CBHW070205100426
42743CB00013B/3061